MAK HEADLINES

Carmel Reilly ❧ Paul Könye

Nelson Thornes

Nelson Thornes

First published in 2007 by Cengage Learning Australia
www.cengage.com.au

This edition published under the imprint of Nelson Thornes Ltd,
Delta Place, 27 Bath Road, Cheltenham, United Kingdom, GL53 7TH

10 9 8 7 6 5 4 3 2
11 10 09 08

Making Headlines
ISBN 978-1-4085-0149-8

Story by Carmel Reilly
Illustrations by Paul Könye
Edited by Cameron Macintosh
Designed by Vonda Pestana
Series Design by James Lowe
Production Controller Seona Galbally
Audio recordings by Juliet Hill, Picture Start
Spoken by Matthew King and Abbe Holmes
Printed in China by 1010 Printing International Ltd

Website www.nelsonthornes.com

MAKING HEADLINES

Carmel Reilly ❦ Paul Könye

Contents

Chapter 1

THE NEWSPAPER

It had been a long hard day
in the classroom,
and Ms Cramble was looking tired.
"Magee," she said, shaking her head,
"you haven't listened to me all day.
I should give you detention ...
but I've got a better idea."

Oh no! I hated it
when she had better ideas.

"I want you to help out
on the school newspaper
for the next month," she said.

"The newspaper!" I groaned.

I might have been full of smart jokes,
but I was pretty bad
at everything else.
What use would I be
on the newspaper?

Working on the newspaper
meant working with Tilly Turner.
Tilly was the editor and reporter
and, unlike me,
she was good at everything.

"Well, Magee, what sort of stories do you think we should be working on, for next week?" Tilly asked me, as we walked over to the newspaper room.

I shrugged.
I never read the newspaper.

8

"So far we have stories on pets,
and the new teacher,
and something on Ms Cramble's
cuckoo clock collection,"
she went on.

"Really?" I said.
It was no wonder I never read
the newspaper.

Just then I saw something
out of the corner of my eye.
It looked like Brad Biggens
sneaking into the office.

"Did you see that?" I hissed at Tilly.

She looked blank.

"And you call yourself a reporter,"
I said, dragging her with me
around the side of the building.

"Look," I whispered,
as Brad came out
with something in his hand.

He quickly pushed whatever it was under his shirt, and ran to the gate.

Before we could see any more, he hopped on his bike and rode off.

Chapter 2

GOOD HEADLINES

"There's a story there!"
I said to Tilly.
"I can see the headlines now:
BAD BRAD IN OFFICE GRAB!"

Tilly stared at me
and shook her head.
"I don't think so, Magee.
Now, I need some help
with the story
about the biscuit baking competition."

"BISCUIT BAKERS TAKE THE CAKE,"
I shouted.

Tilly rolled her eyes.

"Come on, Tilly," I said.
"If we don't have exciting stories,
we could at least have
some good headlines."

13

By Friday afternoon,
I was starting to like working
on the newspaper.
I'd thought up lots of headlines –
although Tilly said
we really had to have stories
to go with them.

I was working on a story
when Tilly flew into
the newspaper room.
"I've seen him again!" she shouted.

Now it was my turn to look blank.
"Who?"

"Brad Biggens," she said.
"You're right, he's up to something.
Quick, get the camera. Let's go."

Tilly was starting to get the idea
of being a reporter.

Chapter 3

FOLLOWING THE STORY

As we raced outside
and around the corner of the library,
we saw Brad walking towards
the back fence.
He was carrying his school jacket,
but there was something about it
that looked strange and heavy.

Tilly and I both stopped.
We could see something was up.

Without saying a word,
we backed around the corner again,
and quietly watched him.

I took the camera out
and took some shots
as he pushed his jacket
into the hedge
at the back of the school grounds.

17

"Looks like he's left something to be picked up," I whispered.

"Let's go and see what it is," said Tilly, as Brad disappeared out of the school gate.

When we got to the hedge,
Tilly bent down and pushed away
some leaves.
There was Brad's jacket,
and wrapped inside were
two notebook computers
from the school office.

Chapter 4

SNAPPED!

It was just after dark when Brad came back to pick up the computers.

He was bending down
to take the jacket
from under the hedge
when he heard us behind him.

He turned to look at us
as my camera flash went off
and I snapped him in the act.

I've never seen anyone look so surprised in my life – especially when Ms Cramble and two police officers stepped out of the darkness.

Tilly rushed forward
with her tape recorder.
"Brad Biggens, do you have
anything to say?"

"I was framed!" he screamed,
as the officers led him away.

"I don't think so!" yelled Tilly.
"We've got photos of you
hiding the notebooks here
this afternoon."

The flash from my next photo lit up
Brad's guilty face.

When I walked into class on Monday,
Ms Cramble was
holding the newspaper.
"Good headline," she said,
giving me a funny smile.

I thought she meant:

**BRAD TAKES NOTES,
POLICE TAKE BRAD**.

But then I saw she was looking
at a different story:

**CLOCK COLLECTOR NOT
SO CUCKOO AFTER ALL.**